TABLE OF CONTENTS

CHRIS TOMLIN

Amazing Grace
(My Chains Are Gone)

Words and Music by JOHN NEWTON, JOHN P. REES
and EDWIN OTHELLO EXCELL
Arrangement and additional chorus by CHRIS TOMLIN
and LOUIE GIGLIO

6

God who called me here below, will be for-ev-er mine, will be for-ev-er mine, You are for-ev-er mine.

Chords Used in This Song

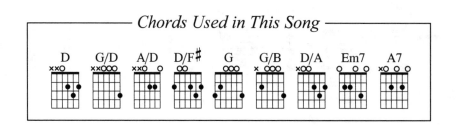

D   G/D   A/D   D/F#   G   G/B   D/A   Em7   A7

Awesome Is The Lord Most High

Words and Music by
CHRIS TOMLIN, JESSE REEVES, CARY PIERCE and JON ABEL

Great are You,___ Lord, might - y___ in strength.___
Where You send___ us, God we___ will go.___

You are faith - ful, and
You're the an - swer, we

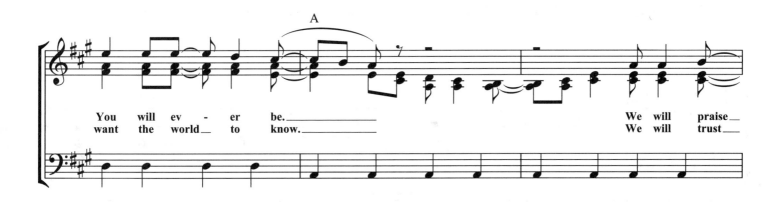

You will ev - er be._____ We will praise___
want the world___ to know._____ We will trust___

___ You all of___ our days,___
___ You when You call___ our name,___

8

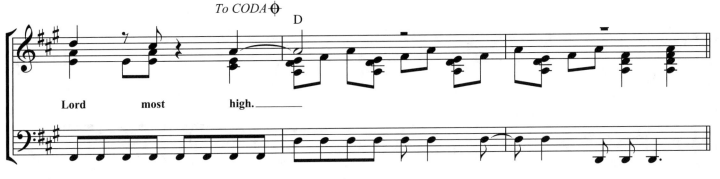

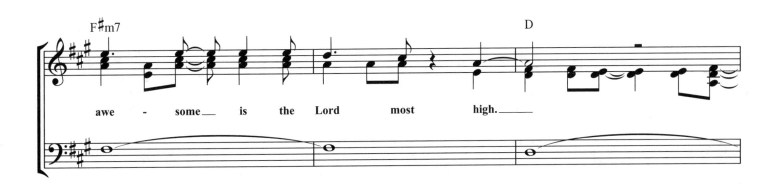

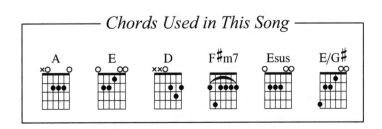

Chords Used in This Song

Enough

**Words and Music by
CHRIS TOMLIN and LOUIS GIGLIO**

Everlasting God

Medium Rock ♩ = 98

Words and Music by
BRENTON BROWN and KEN RILEY

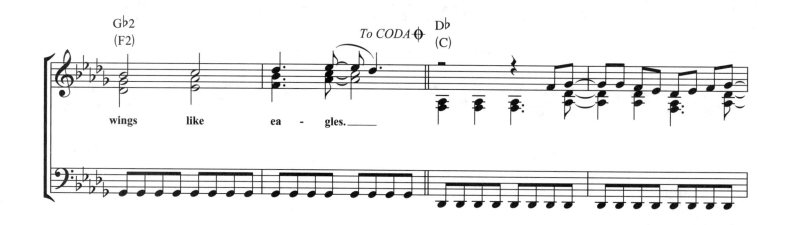

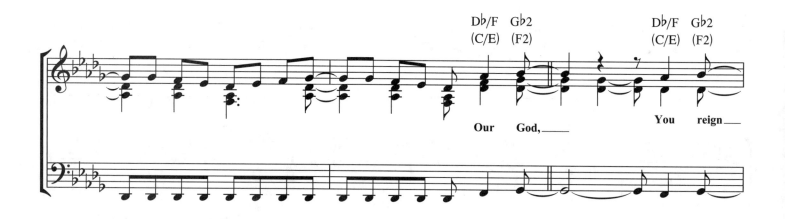

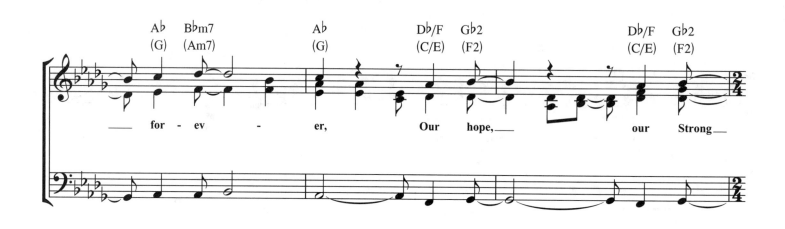

rit.

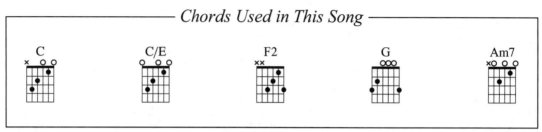

Chords Used in This Song

C   C/E   F2   G   Am7

Glorious

**Words and Music by
CHRIS TOMLIN and JESSE REEVES**

We lift our hands in praise to You, We lift our

hearts in wor - ship to You, Lord.

We lift our voice to You and sing, Our great-est

love will ev - er be You, Lord.

Maj - es - ty and pow - er,___

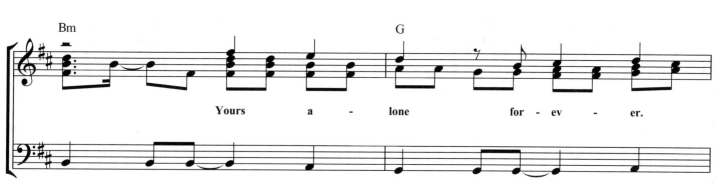

Yours a - lone for - ev - er.

Maj - es - ty and pow - er___

Yours___ a - lone___ for - ev - er___

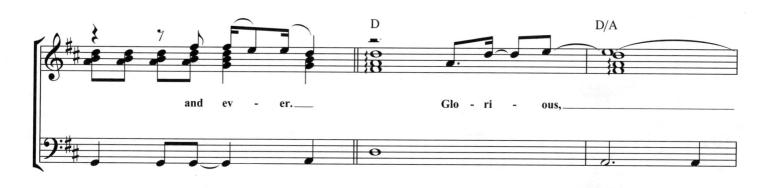

and ev - er.___ Glo - ri - ous,___

CODA

Chords Used in This Song

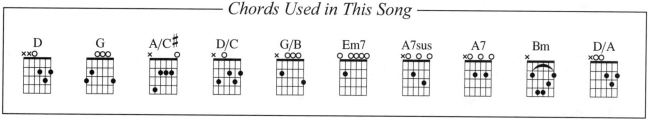

Glory In The Highest

Words and Music by
CHRIS TOMLIN, ED CASH, MATT REDMAN,
JESSE REEVES and DANIEL CARSON

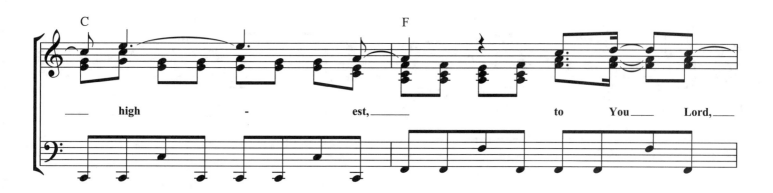

high - est,_____ to You____ Lord,____

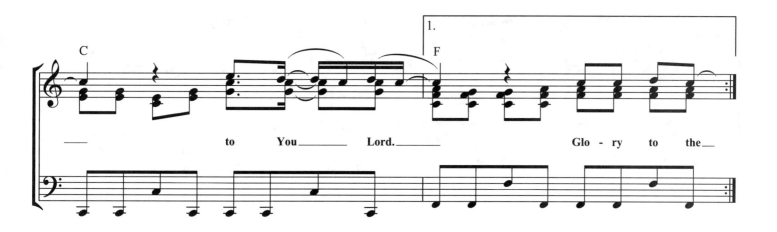

____ to You_____ Lord._____ Glo - ry to the__

____ All the earth__ will sing____ Your praise,__ the moon__

__ and stars,__ the sun__ and rain.__ Ev - 'ry na - tion will__ pro - claim,__ that You__

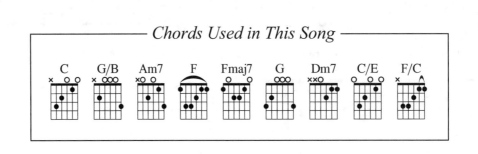

Chords Used in This Song

How Can I Keep From Singing

Words and Music by
CHRIS TOMLIN, MATT REDMAN
and ED CASH

sing.   Yeah,_____   I can__

_____ sing._____

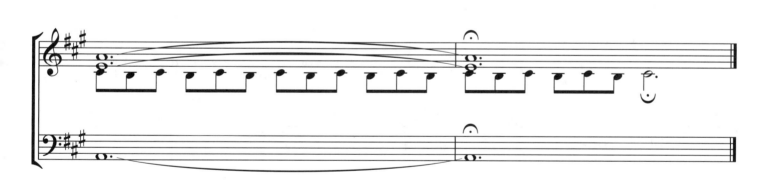

Chords Used in This Song

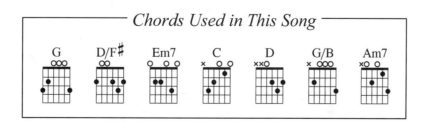

Let God Arise

**Words and Music by
CHRIS TOMLIN, ED CASH
and JESSE REEVES**

Hear the ho - ly roar of God re - sound,
(His en) - e - mies will run for sure,

Watch the wa - ters part be - fore us now.
The church will stand, She will en - dure.

Come and see what He has done
He holds the keys of life,

for us, Tell the world of His great love,
our Lord, Death has no sting, no fi - nal word, Our God

Our___ God reigns_____ now and for-ev - er, He reigns___

___ now and for-ev - er. God__ a - rise___ er._____

Play 4 times

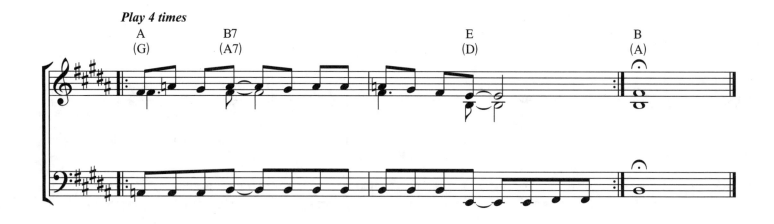

Chords Used In This Song

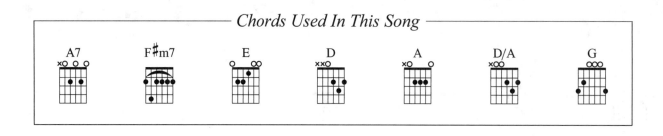

Let Your Mercy Rain

Words and Music by
CHRIS TOMLIN, ED CASH and JESSE REEVES

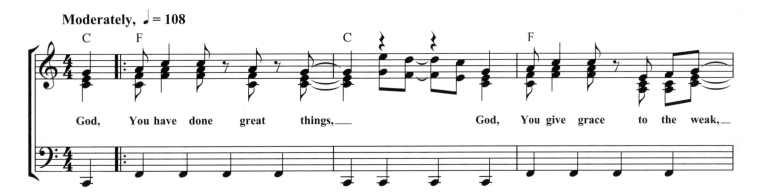

God, You have done great things, ___ God, You give grace to the weak, ___

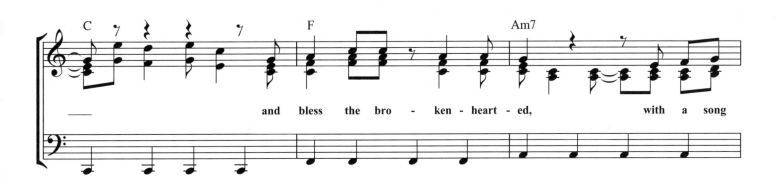

___ and bless the bro - ken - heart - ed, with a song

of praise ___ to sing. ___ You reached down and lift - ed us up,

You came ___ run - ning, look - ing for us. And now there's

when my world's___ fall - ing a - part.___ So let Your

mer - cy rain, let Your mer - cy rain_____ on___ us.___

Let it rain.

Repeat and fade

Chords Used in This Song

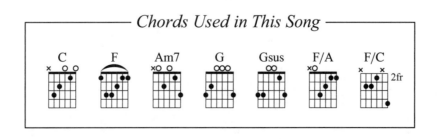

C   F   Am7   G   Gsus   F/A   F/C

The Lion Became The Lamb

**Words and Music by
MATT MAHER and CHRIS TOMLIN**

Made To Worship

Words and Music by
CHRIS TOMLIN, STEPHAN SHARP
and ED CASH

You and I,_____ _____ you and I_____

yeah,_____ _____ yeah,_____ oo._____

We_____ were meant_____ to be._____

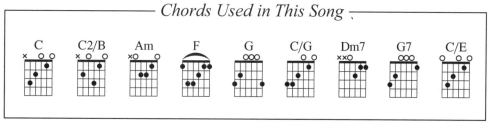

Chords Used in This Song

Over Me

Words and Music by
CHRIS TOMLIN and SETH WALKER

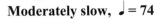

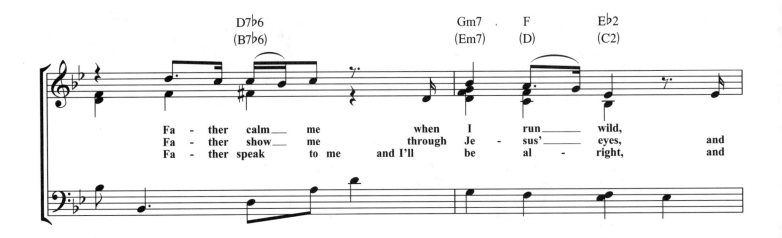

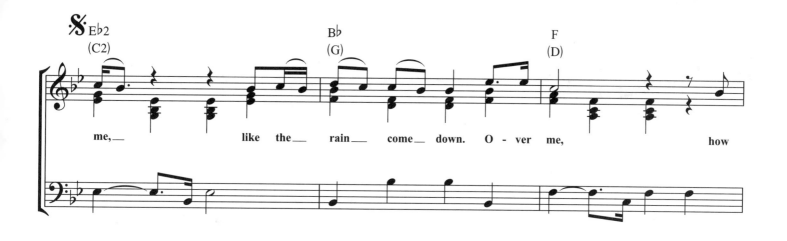

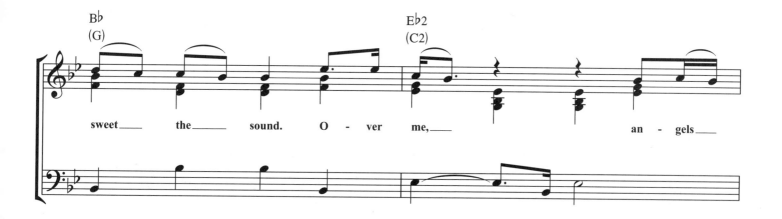

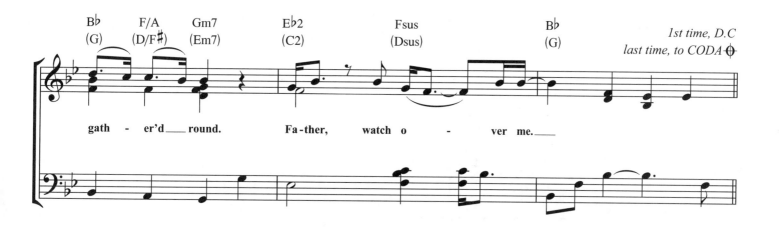

O - ver

Fa- ther,   watch o -   ver me.

Chords Used in This Song

G   C/G   D   B7b6   Em7   C2   D/F#   Dsus

Rejoice

**Words and Music by
CHRIS TOMLIN, ED CASH
and JESSE REEVES**

Moderately ♩ = 96

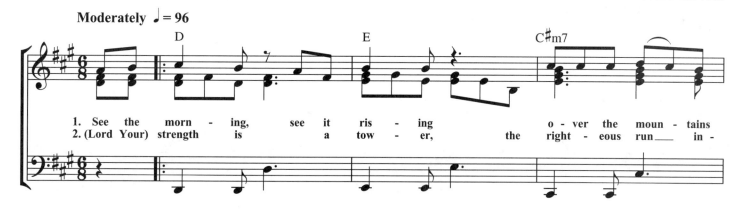

1. See the morn - ing, see it ris - ing   o - ver the moun - tains
2. (Lord Your) strength is a tow - er, the right - eous run___ in -

high.   See the mer - cy in the might - y hand of
to.   Lord Your love is a ban - ner o - ver

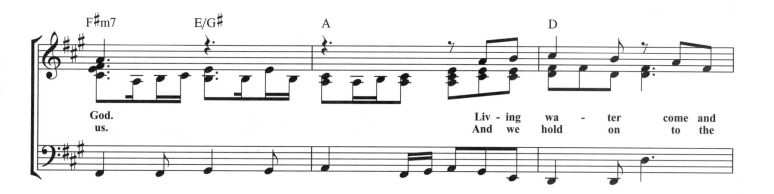

God.   Liv - ing wa - ter come and
us.   And we hold on to the

fill us, on - ly You can sat - is - fy. Turn our
prom - ise, that Your hold on us___ is true. There's no

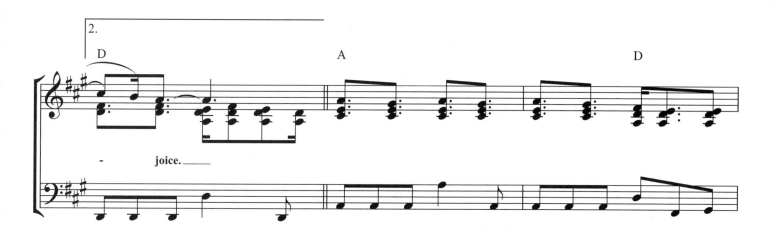

D
2. D
D.S. al CODA
CODA
D
Lord Your - joice.
- joice.
D
E
Al - ways, a - gain I say re -
C♯m7
F♯m7
joice. Al - ways, a -
D
gain I say re - joice. Al -
E
C♯m7
ways, a - gain I say re - joice.

joice.

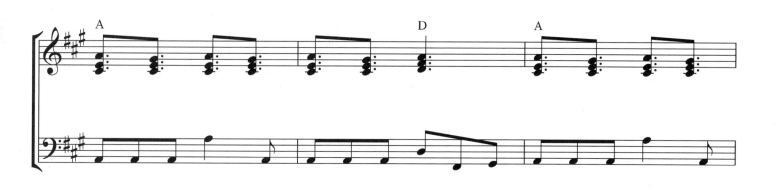

Chords Used in This Song

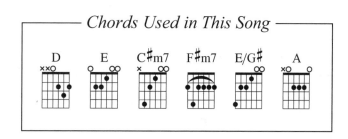

Uncreated One

Words and Music by
CHRIS TOMLIN and J.D. WALT

72

Chords Used in This Song

Enough

Words and Music by
CHRIS TOMLIN and **LOUIS GIGLIO**

Made To Worship

Moderately ♩ = 86

Words and Music by
CHRIS TOMLIN, STEPHAN SHARP and ED CASH

Capo 4 (G)

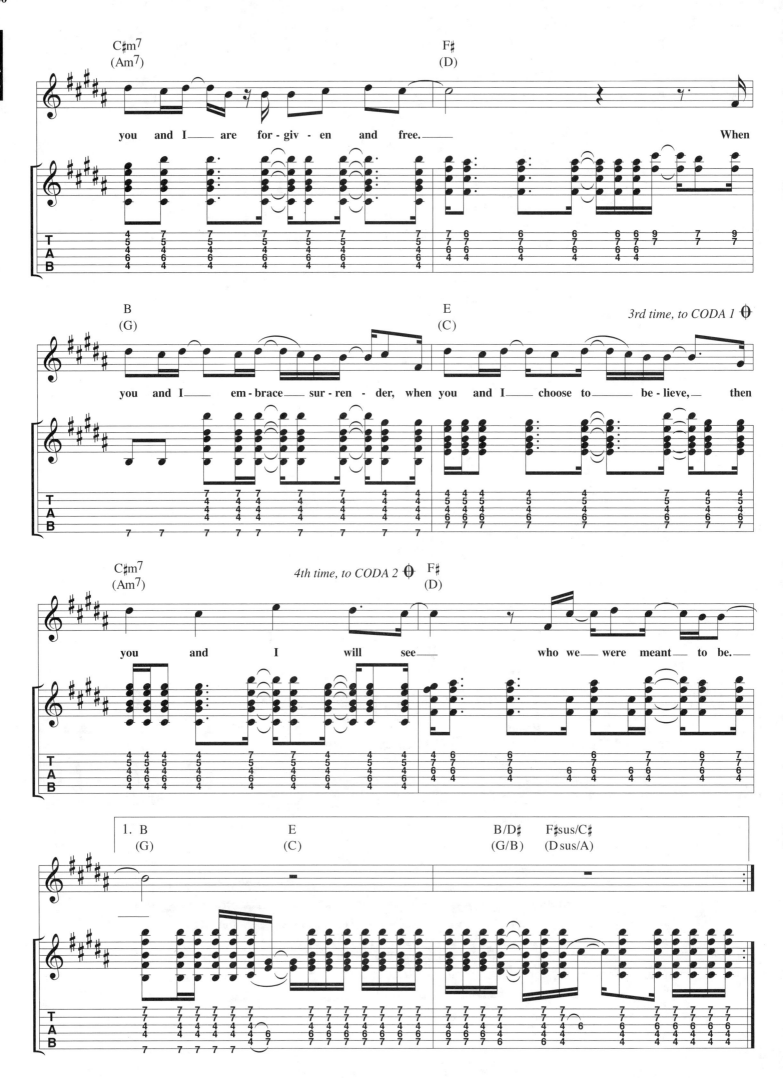

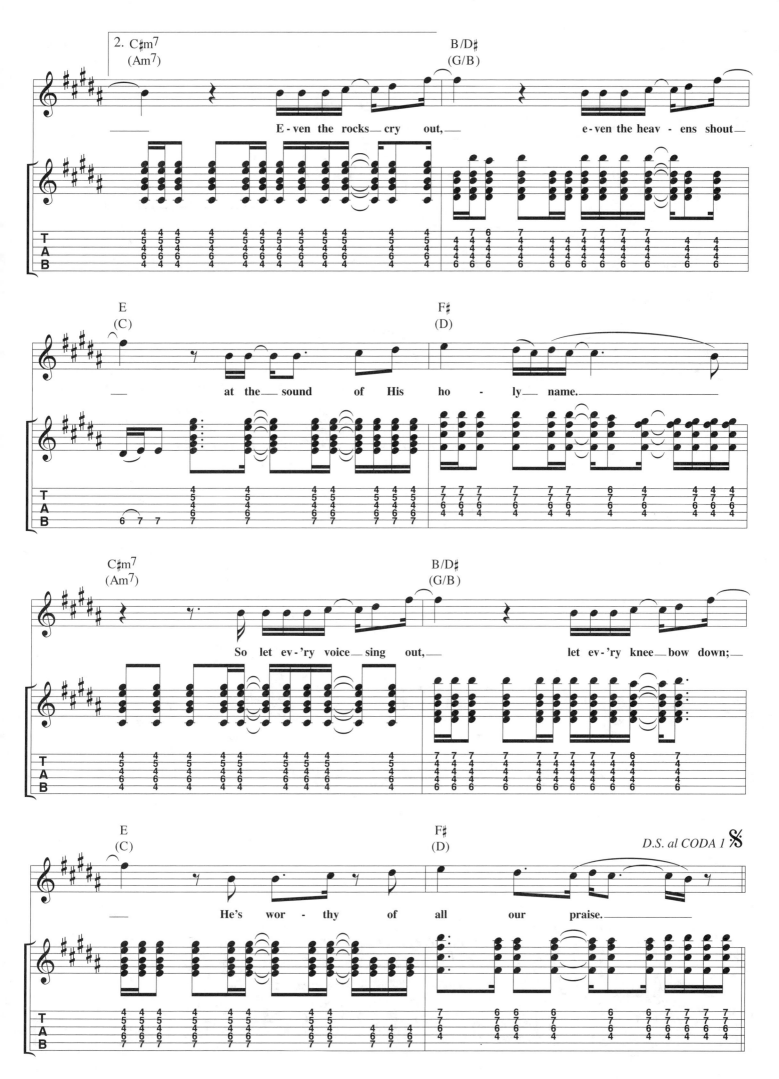

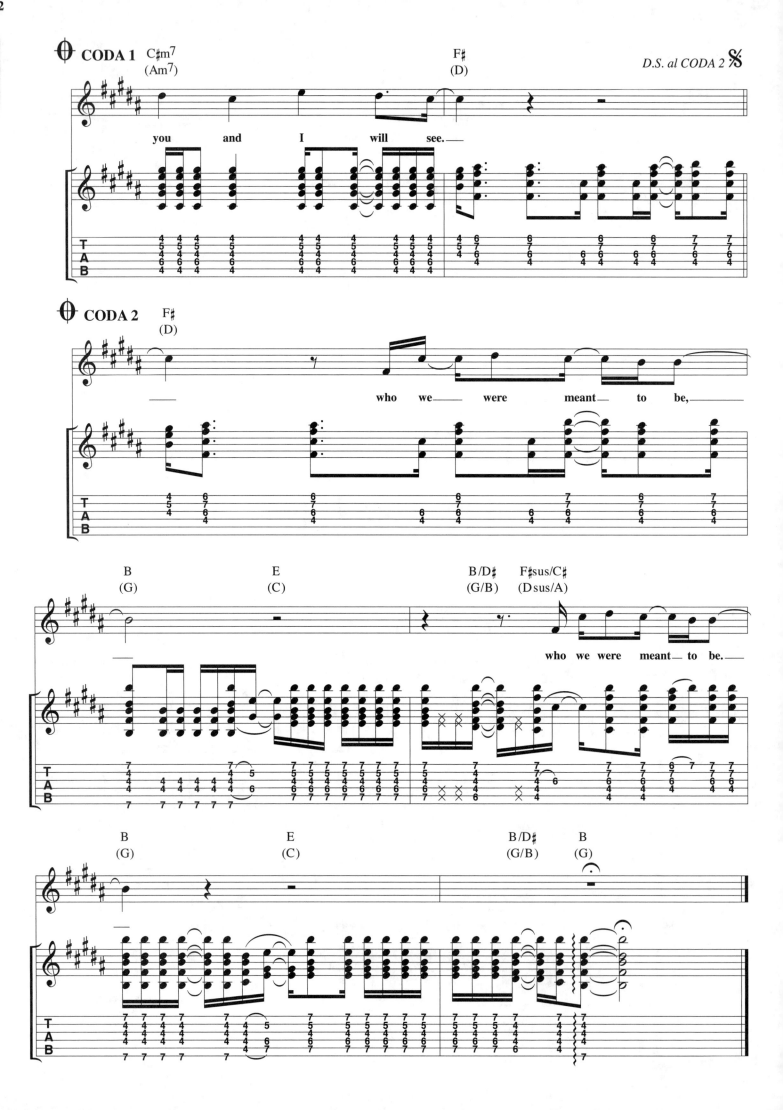

How Can I Keep From Singing

Words and Music by
CHRIS TOMLIN, MATT REDMAN and ED CASH

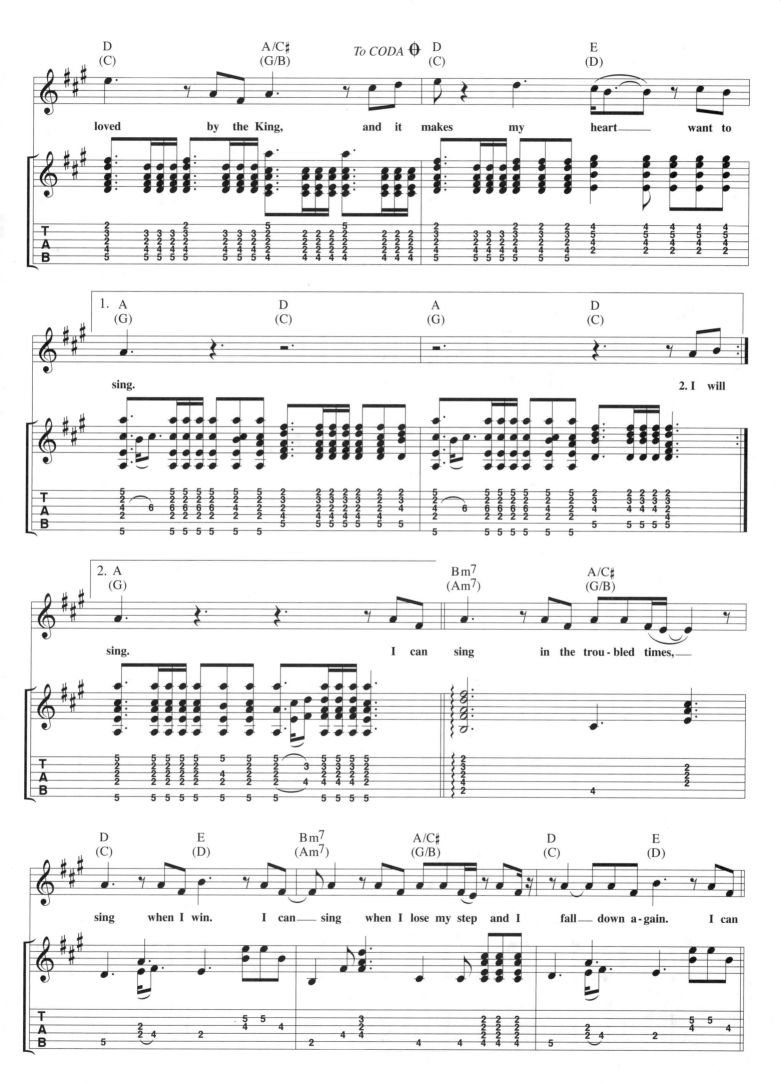

86

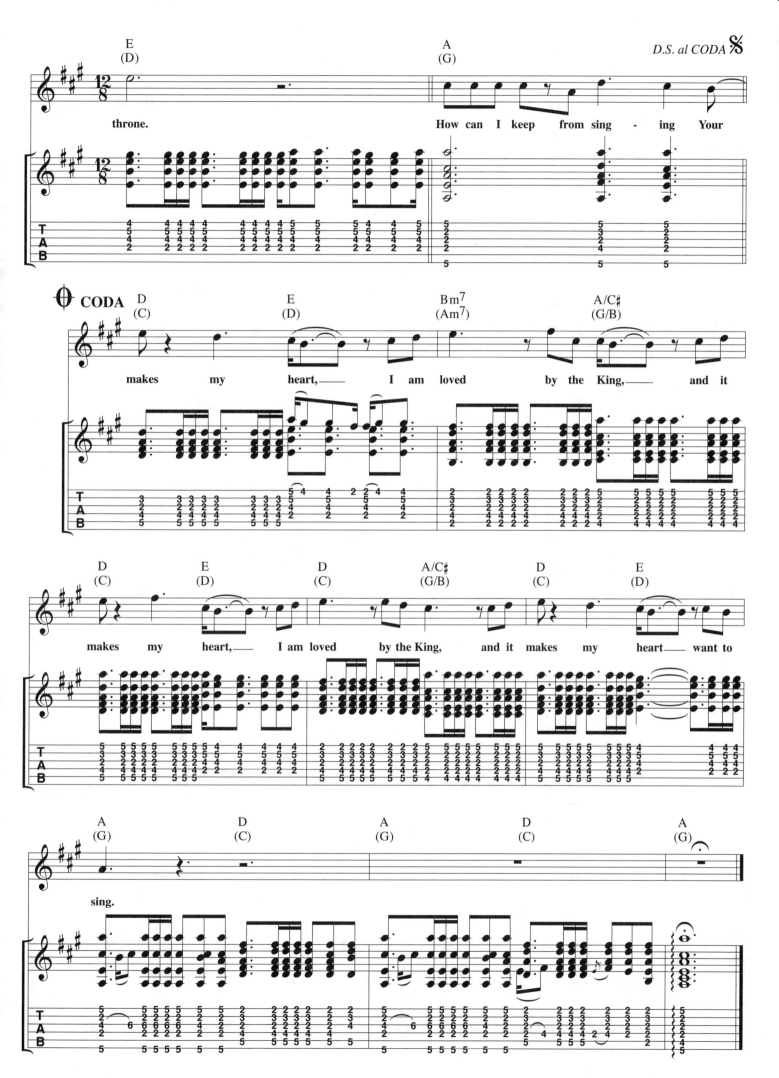

Over Me

Words and Music by
CHRIS TOMLIN and SETH WALKER

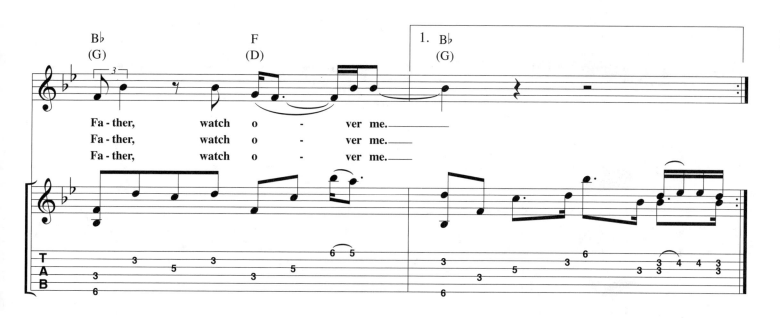

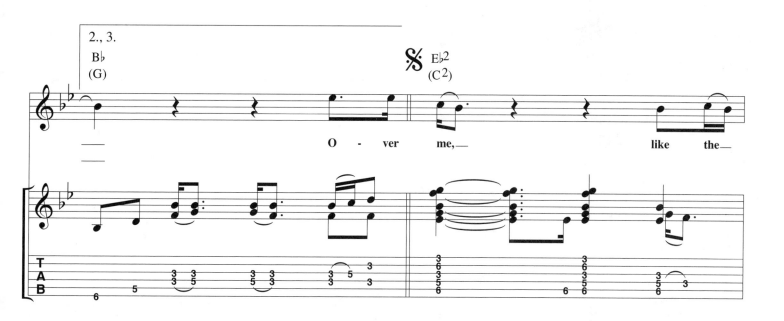

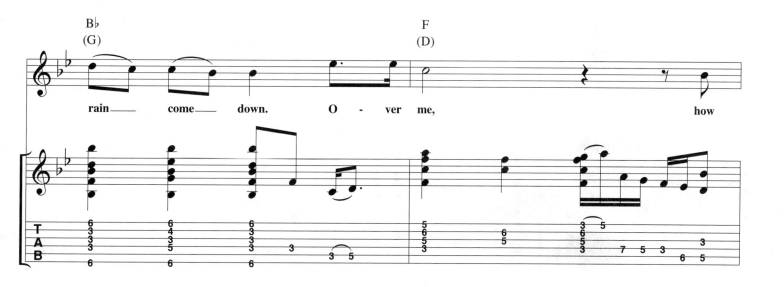

TAB

The Lion Became The Lamb

Words and Music by
MATT MAHER and CHRIS TOMLIN

Moderately ♩ = 76

Capo 1 (C)

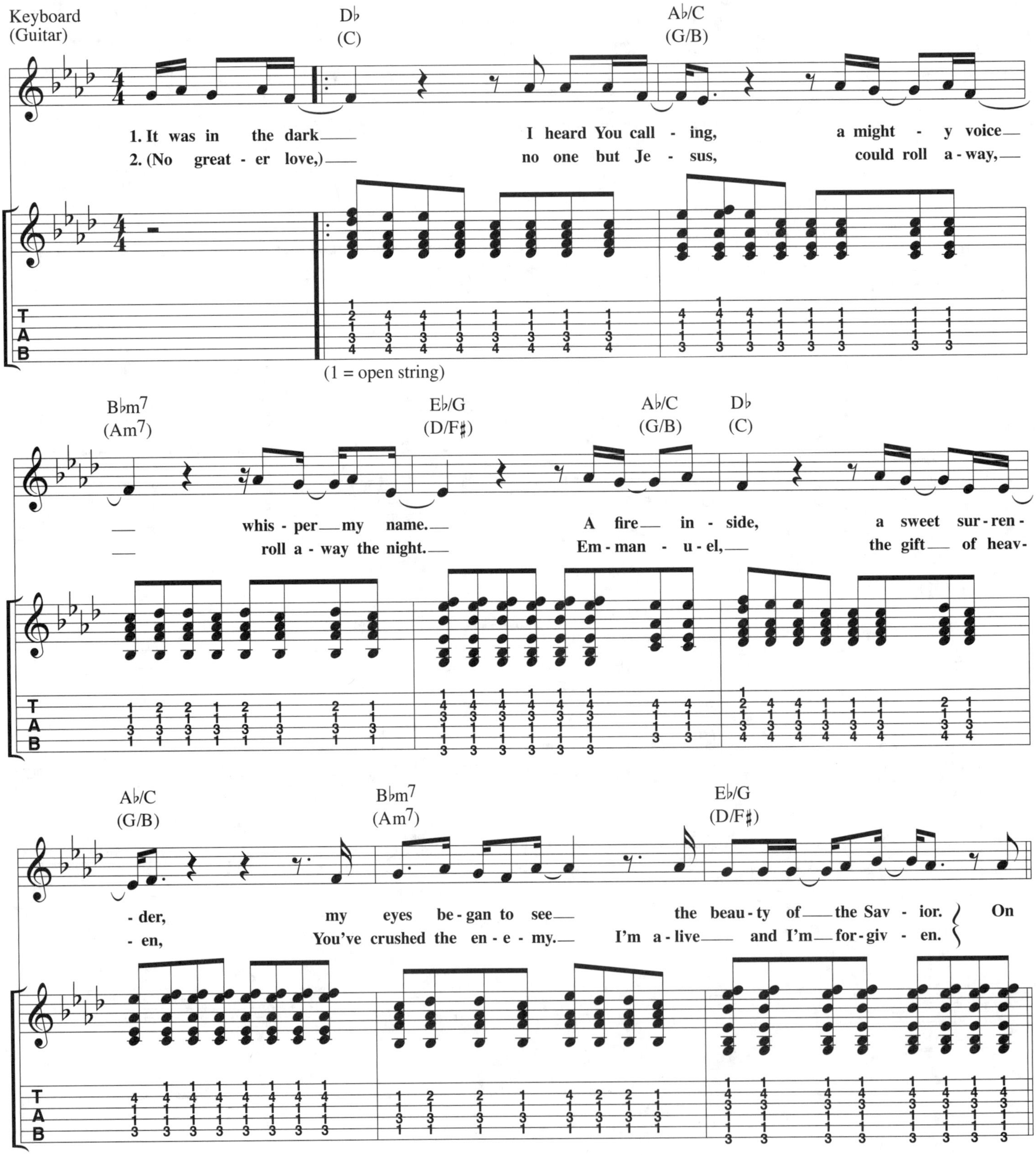

Keyboard
(Guitar)
D♭
(C)
A♭/C
(G/B)
1. It was in the dark I heard You call - ing, a might - y voice
2. (No great - er love,) no one but Je - sus, could roll a - way,
(1 = open string)
B♭m7
(Am7)
E♭/G
(D/F♯)
A♭/C
(G/B)
D♭
(C)
whis - per my name. A fire in - side, a sweet sur - ren -
roll a - way the night. Em - man - u - el, the gift of heav -
A♭/C
(G/B)
B♭m7
(Am7)
E♭/G
(D/F♯)
- der, my eyes be - gan to see the beau - ty of the Sav - ior. On
- en, You've crushed the en - e - my. I'm a - live and I'm for - giv - en.

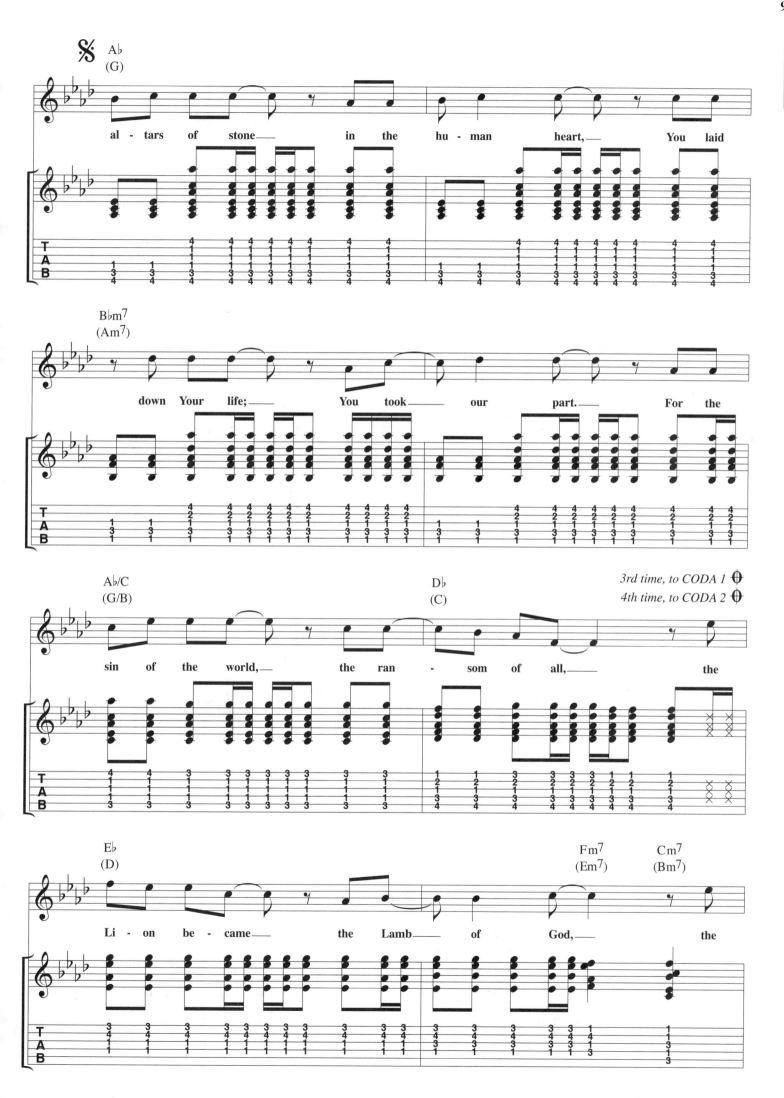

94

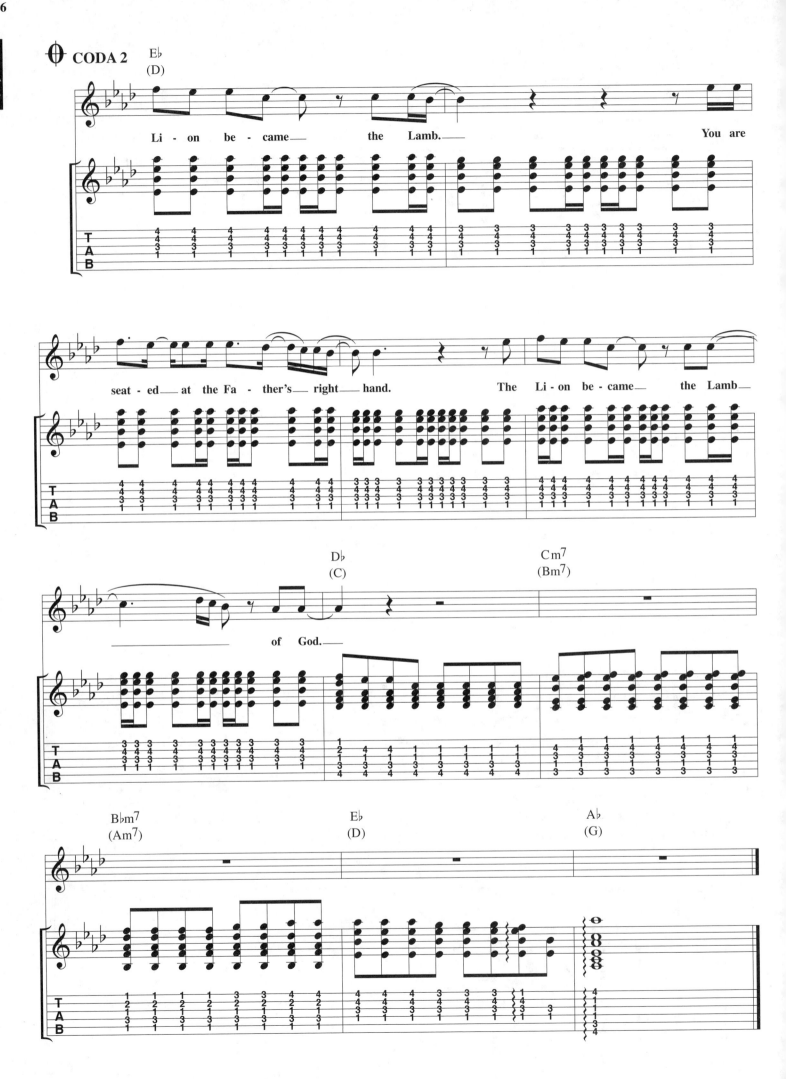

How Can I Keep From Singing

On the last day of the Chris Tomlin Indescribable Tour, Matt showed Chris an old Hymn from 1860 written by Robert Lowery. Chris wanted to adapt this hymn into a modern song. The main lyric from the hymn was "How can I keep from singing," which of course, became the title of the song.

Enough

I still remember Louie handing me a torn piece of paper from his journal just before the 2001 Passion tour was to hit the road. On it was written this thought among others; "all of You is more than enough for all of me... for every thirst...for every need." I thought this was such an important and refreshing truth. A truth not just for an audience, but a truth for me personally. Let's face it, we live in a broken world and we live broken lives. That's why I love Psalm 103, v.1-5 "Praise the Lord, O my soul, all my inmost being, praise His holy name. Praise the Lord, O my soul, and forget not all His benefits...who forgives all your sins and heals all your diseases, who redeems your life from the pit and crowns you with love and compassion, who satisfies your desires with good things so that your youth is renewed like the eagle's."

God is enough! Way more than enough! In your loneliest and most broken times, He is the one who satisfies.

See the morning...Our God is as faithful as the rising sun.
"Because of the Lord's great love we are not consumed,
for his compassions never fail. They are new every morning;
great is your faithfulness."   Lamentations 3:22-23

"Listen to my cry for help, my King
and my God, for to You I pray. In the
morning, O Lord, You hear my voice;
in the morning I lay my requests
before You and wait in expectation."
Psalm 5:2-3

ENOUGH

All of You is more than enough for all of me
For every thirst and every need
You satisfy me with Your love
And all I have in You is more than enough

You are my supply
My breath of life
And still more awesome than I know
You are my reward
Worth living for
And still more awesome than I know

You're my sacrifice
Of greatest price
And still more awesome than I know
You're the coming King
You are everything
And still more awesome than I know

More than all I want
More than all I need
You are more than enough for me
More than all I know
More than all I can see
You are more than enough

Written by Chris Tomlin and Louie Giglio

HOW CAN I KEEP FROM SINGING?

There is an endless song
It echoes in my soul / I hear the music ring

And though the storms may come
I am holding on / To the rock I cling

How can I keep from singing Your praise?
How can I ever say enough?
How amazing is Your love?
How can I keep from shouting Your name?
I know I am loved by the King
And it makes my heart want to sing

I will lift my eyes / In the darkest night / For I know my Savior lives

And I will walk with You / Knowing You'll see me through
And sing the songs You give

I can sing in the troubled times
Sing when I win
I can sing when I lose my step
And fall down again
I can sing 'cause You pick me up
Sing 'cause You're there
I can sing 'cause You hear me, Lord
When I call to You in prayer
I can sing with my last breath
Sing for I know
That I'll sing with the angels
And the saints around the throne

Written by Chris Tomlin, Matt Redman and Ed Cash

MADE TO WORSHIP

Before the day / Before the light
Before the world revolved around the sun
God on high / Stepped down into time
And wrote the story of His love
for everyone

He has filled our hearts with wonder
So that we always remember

You and I were made to worship
You and I are called to love
You and I are forgiven and free
When you and I embrace surrender
When you and I choose to believe
Then you and I will see
who we were meant to be

All we are / And all we have
Is all a gift from God that we receive
Brought to life
We open up our eyes
To see the majesty and glory of the King

He has filled our hearts with wonder
So that we always remember

Even the rocks cry out
Even the heavens shout
At the sound of His Holy name
So let every voice sing out
Let every knee bow down
He is worthy of all our praise

Written by Chris Tomlin, Stephan Sharp and Ed Cash

"VERY EARLY IN THE MORNING, WHILE IT WAS STILL
DARK, JESUS GOT UP, LEFT THE HOUSE AND WENT OFF
TO A SOLITARY PLACE, WHERE HE PRAYED." MARK 1:35

"The people walking in darkness have seen
a great light; on those living in the land of the
shadow of death a light has dawned."
Isaiah 9:2

LION BECAME THE LAMB

It was in the dark I heard you calling
A mighty voice whisper my name
A fire inside, a sweet surrender
My eyes began to see the beauty of the Savior

On altars of stone in the human heart
You laid down Your life; You took our part
For the sin of the world, the ransom of all
The Lion became the Lamb of God
The Lion became the Lamb of God

No greater love, no one but Jesus
Could roll away, roll away the night
Emmanuel, the gift of heaven
You've Crushed the enemy
Now I'm alive and (I'm) forgiven

And the time had come,
though the war was won
The battle for my freedom had just begun
But You wouldn't abandon me
for the sake of Your story

Written by Chris Tomlin and Matt Maher

OVER ME

Father hold me
Like a new born child
Father hold me
Like a new born child
Father calm me
When I run wild
Father, watch over me

Father cool me
When the fever's high
Father cool me
When the fever's high
Father show me
Through Jesus' eyes
Father, watch over me

Over me
Like the rain come down
Over me
How sweet the sound
Over me
Angels gathered round
Father, watch over me

Father call me
To Your loving side
Father call me
To Your loving side
Father speak to me
And I'll be alright
Father, watch over me

Written by Chris Tomlin and Seth Walker

Jesus is the Light of the World,
the Bright and Morning Star!

Let God arise!

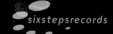

Made To Worship

Stephan Sharp, Ed Cash's assistant, had written this amazing chorus, and showed it to Ed, who sent it to Chris. Chris loved the song and thought that it spoke so much truth. Chris immediately went to the scriptures and wrote the verses straight out of the Bible about how amazing the glory and wonder of Almighty God can be.

Psalm 148.
¹Praise the LORD!
  Praise the LORD from the heavens;
  Praise Him in the heights!
²Praise Him, all His angels;
  Praise Him, all His hosts!
³Praise Him, sun and moon;
  Praise Him, all stars of light!
⁴Praise Him, highest heavens,
  And the waters that are above the heavens!
⁵Let them praise the name of the LORD,
  For He commanded and they were created.
⁶He has also established them forever and ever;
  He has made a decree which will not pass away.
⁷Praise the LORD from the earth,
  Sea monsters and all deeps;
⁸Fire and hail, snow and clouds;
  Stormy wind, fulfilling His word;
⁹Mountains and all hills;
  Fruit trees and all cedars;
¹⁰Beasts and all cattle;
  Creeping things and winged fowl;
¹¹Kings of the earth and all peoples;
  Princes and all judges of the earth;
¹²Both young men and virgins;
  Old men and children.
¹³Let them praise the name of the LORD,
  For His name alone is exalted;
  His glory is above earth and heaven.
¹⁴And He has lifted up a horn for His people,
  Praise for all His godly ones;
  Even for the sons of Israel, a people near to Him.
  Praise the LORD!

God was so intentional when He made us.
We were made to worship Him and Him alone!
Exodus tells us that we are to have no other gods before Him and to worship NOTHING but Him.

Lion Became The Lamb

Matt Maher writes:
"Originally, this song was intended to be a part of the musical project that accompanied the Narnia movie, The Lion, The Witch, and The Wardrobe. The more I unpacked the character's personalities and what they represented in the story; I was repeatedly drawn to Edmund. He wasn't the brave older brother, or the courageous, daring older sister or even the sweet and innocent Lucy. Rather, he was the sibling who sold his family out in exchange for his own pleasures. As you may know, it's thought that the lamppost in the story might represent the light of Christ, hence the lyrics emulating Edmund' decisions, "...it was in the dark far from the lamp light I was drawn deep into the night." The pre-chorus and second verse speaks to Edmund's conversation with Aslan. For Edmund, his whole transformation occurs out of a decision he makes. In my mind, the chorus is an allegory for the cross, "...on alters of stone / in the human heart / you laid down your life you took our part / for the sins of the world / a ransom for all / the Lion became the Lamb of God." Chris Tomlin was introduced to the song by a mutual friend of ours and really gravitated to the chorus and saw it as having a very congregational feel. He decided to tweak some of the lyric for example "...it was in the dark that I heard you calling, a mighty voice whisper my name." With Chris' rewrites and the relatable subject matte of the song, this one seems to really touch the core of describing our humanity, and hopefully draws the participant and the worship leader to also focus on the beautiful sacrifice Christ made for us."

Over Me

Chris fell in love with this song when a friend & local musician Seth Walker, from Ausin, TX, played this song for him. The simple repetitive style of this song made it perfect for a stripped-down acoustic cut at the end of the special edition album.

Amazing Grace (My Chains Are Gone)

Words and Music by JOHN NEWTON, JOHN P. REES and EDWIN OTHELLO EXCELL
Arrangement and additional chorus by CHRIS TOMLIN and LOUIE GIGLIO

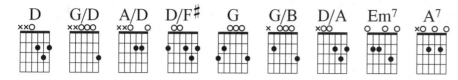

D   G/D   A/D   D/F#   G   G/B   D/A   Em7   A7

Capo 3 (D)

CONTINUED...

VERSE 1:

D   G/D   D
Amaz - ing Grace, how   sweet the sound,

                          A/D
That saved a wretch like   me.

        D   D/F#   G   D
I once   was lost, but now   I'm found,

              A/D   D
Was blind but now   I   see.

VERSE 2:

        D   G/D   D
'Twas Grace that taught my heart to fear,

                      A/D
And Grace my fears re   -   lieved.

        D   D/F#   G   D
How pre - cious did that Grace   appear,

              A/D   D
The hour I first believed.

CHORUS:

      D/F#   G   D/F#
My   chains are   gone, I've been set   free,

              G/B   D/A
My God, my Savior has ransomed   me.

      D/F#   G   D/F#
And like   a flood His mercy   reigns,

              Em7   A7   D
Unending love,   Amazing Grace.

VERSE 3:

        D   G/D   D
The Lord   has promised good   to me,

                          A/D
His word my hope secures.

        D   D/F#   G   D
He will   my   shield and por - tion be,

              A/D   D
As long as   life endures.

(REPEAT CHORUS TWICE)

VERSE 4:

G/D   D   G/D   D
    The earth   shall soon dissolve   like snow,

                          A/D
The sun forbear to shine.

        D   D/F#   G   D
But   God who called me here   below,

              A/D   D
Will be for - ever mine,

              A/D   D
Will be for - ever mine,

              A/D   D
You are for - ever   mine.

Awesome Is The Lord Most High

CHRIS TOMLIN, JESSE REEVES, CARY PIERCE and JON ABEL

KEY OF (A)

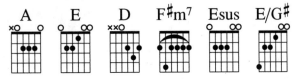

CONTINUED...

VERSE 1:

A   E
 Great are You, Lord, mighty in strength.

D
 You are faithful, and You will ever be.

A   E
 We will praise You all of our days,

D   F#m7
 It's for Your glory, we offer everything.

CHORUS 1:

(Esus)* A   *1st & 2nd time only*
 Raise your hands all you nations,

    D
Shout to God all creation,

  F#m7   D
How awesome is the Lord most high.

VERSE 2:

A   E
 Where You send us, God we will go.

D
 You're the answer, we want the world to know.

A   E
 We will trust You when You call our name,

D   F#m7
 Where You lead us, we'll follow all the way.

(REPEAT CHORUS 1)

CHORUS 2:

      A
We will praise You together,

  E/G#
For now and forever.

  F#m7   D
How awesome is the Lord most high.

BRIDGE:

A   E
Hallelujah, hallelujah,

  F#m7   D
How awesome is the Lord most high.

A   E/G#
Hallelujah, hallelujah,

  F#m7   D
How awesome is the Lord most high.

(REPEAT CHORUS 1 & 2 TWICE)

A E/G# F#m7 D

Enough

CHRIS TOMLIN and LOUIE GIGLIO

G	C²	Dsus	G/B	Am⁷	C²/E

Capo 2 (G)

VERSE 1:

G   C²   Dsus
   You are my   supply,

      G/B   C²
my breath   of life;

        Am⁷   Dsus
Still more awe   -   some than I know.

G   C²   Dsus
   You are my   reward,

      G/B   C²
worth liv   -   ing for;

        Am⁷   Dsus
Still more awe   -   some than I know.

CHORUS:

        G   C²/E   Dsus
And all of You is more than enough

    C²   G
for   all of me,

C²/E   Dsus   C²   G
For every thirst   and   every need.

   C²/E   Dsus   C²   G/B
You   satisfy   me   with Your love,

   C²   Dsus
And all I have in You

CHORUS TAG:

is more than enough.
(G   C²/E   Dsus   C²   G   C²/E   Dsus   C²)
                           1st time only

VERSE 2:

G²   C²   Dsus
   You're my sac - rifice

      G/B   C²
of great   -   est price;

        Am⁷   Dsus
Still more awe - some than I know.

G   C²   Dsus
   You're the com - ing King,

      G/B   C²
You are ev   -   erything;

        Am⁷   Dsus
Still more awe   -   some than I know.

CONTINUED...

(REPEAT CHORUS & CHORUS TAG)

BRIDGE:

G   C²   Dsus
   More than all   I want,

          C²   G/B
more than all   I need,

C²   Dsus
   You are more   than enough for me.

G   C²
   More than all   I know,

Dsus   C²   G/B
   more than all   I can,

C²   Dsus
   You are more   than enough.

(REPEAT CHORUS)

ENDING:

G/B   C²   Dsus
   And all I have in You,   Lord,

G/B   C²   Dsus
   All I have in You

                  G   C²/E   Dsus
is more than enough,

C²   G   C²/E   Dsus   C²
more than enough.

G   C²/E   Dsus   C²

G   C²/E   Dsus   C²   G

Everlasting God

BRENTON BROWN and KEN RILEY

C   C/E   F² G   Am⁷

Capo 1 (C)

VERSE:

C
  Strength will rise as we wait upon the Lord,

We will wait upon the Lord,

We will wait upon the Lord.

Strength will rise as we wait upon the Lord,

We will wait upon the Lord,

We will wait upon the Lord.

PRE-CHORUS:

C/E   F²   C/E   F²   G   Am⁷   G
Our   God, You   reign for - ev - er,

C/E   F²   C/E   F²   G   Am⁷   G
Our   hope, our   Strong De - liver - er.

CHORUS 1:

C
  You are the everlasting God,

F²
  The everlasting God,

Am⁷
  You do not faint,

    F²
You won't grow weary.

INSTRUMENTAL:

C

CONTINUED...

(REPEAT VERSE)

(REPEAT PRE-CHORUS)

(REPEAT CHORUS 1)

CHORUS 2:

C
  You're the defender of the weak,

F²
  You comfort those in need,

Am⁷
  You lift us up

    F²
On wings like eagles.

(REPEAT INSTRUMENTAL)

(REPEAT PRE-CHORUS)

(REPEAT CHORUS 1 & 2)

ENDING:

C   F²   Am⁷
  From ev - erlasting, to ev   -   erlasting,

              F²
'Cause you are ev - erlasting.

C

Glorious

CHRIS TOMLIN and JESSE REEVES

KEY OF (D)

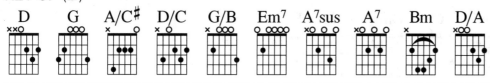

CONTINUED...

VERSE 1:

D
   We lift our hands in praise to You,

                                     G
We lift our hearts in worship to You, Lord.

            D
We lift our voice to You and sing,

                              G
Our greatest love will ever be You, Lord. You, Lord!

CHORUS 1:

D   A/C♯ D/C   G/B
  Glorious,   over us,

Em⁷   A⁷sus A⁷ D
  You shall reign   glo - rious.

VERSE 2:

D
   There is a King that we adore,

                             G
With humble hearts we bow before You, Lord.

            D
There is a place we long to be,

                      G
Face to face we long to see You, Lord. You, Lord!

(REPEAT CHORUS 2 TWICE)

BRIDGE:

Bm   G
   Majes - ty and power,

Bm   G
   Are Yours a - lone forever,

Bm   G
   Majes - ty and power,

Bm   G
   Are Yours a - lone forever and ever.

CHORUS 2:

D   D/A D/C   G/B
  Glorious,   over us,

Em⁷   A⁷sus A⁷ D
  You shall reign   glo - rious.

(REPEAT CHORUS 2 THREE TIMES)

ENDING:

D   A/C♯   D/C   G/B

Em⁷   A⁷sus A⁷ D

Glory In The Highest

CHRIS TOMLIN, ED CASH, MATT REDMAN, JESSE REEVES and DANIEL CARSON

KEY OF (C)

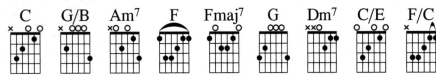

C   G/B   Am⁷   F   Fmaj⁷   G   Dm⁷   C/E   F/C

CONTINUED...

VERSE 1:

C   G/B
   You are the first,   You go before,

Am⁷   F
   You are the last,   Lord You're the encore.

C   G/B
   Your name's in lights   for all to see,

Am⁷   F
   The starry host   declare Your glory.

CHORUS 1:

           Fmaj⁷   G
Glory in the highest,

           Am⁷   G
Glory in the highest,

           Dm⁷   C/E   F
Glory in the highest.

VERSE 2:

C   G/B
   Apart from You   there is no God,

Am⁷
   Light of the world,

F
   the bright and morning star.

C   G/B
   Your name will shine   for all to see,

Am⁷   F
   You are the one,   You are my glory.

(REPEAT CHORUS 1)

BRIDGE:

G   Am⁷
   And no one else

              F   G
could ever compare   to You, Lord.

          Am⁷   F
All the earth   together declare:

CHORUS 2:

                C   F
Glory in the   highest,

                C   F
Glory in the   highest,

                C   F
Glory in the   highest,

          C   F
to You Lord,   to You Lord.

(REPEAT CHORUS 2)

ENDING:

C
All the earth will sing Your praise,

              F
The moon   and stars, the sun and rain.

       C
Ev - 'ry nation will proclaim,

          F
That You   are God and You will ransom.

C
Glory, glory Hallelujah,

F
Glory, glory to You Lord.

C   F
Glory, glory Hallelujah,   Hallelujah.

C   F/C   C   F/C

How Can I Keep From Singing

CHRIS TOMLIN, MATT REDMAN and ED CASH

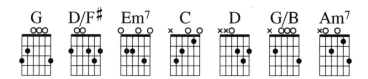

G   D/F♯   Em⁷   C   D   G/B   Am⁷

Capo 2 (G)

VERSE 1:

         G   D/F♯
There is an endless song, echoes in my soul,

  Em⁷   C
I hear the music ring.

     D   G   D/F♯
And though the storms may come, I am holding on,

Em⁷   D/F♯   G   Em⁷   C
To   the   rock   I   cling.

CHORUS:

G   D
How can I keep from singing Your   praise?

          C   G/B
How can I ever say e - nough,

       C   D
How a - mazing is Your   love?

G   D
How can I keep from shouting Your   name?

         C   G/B
I know I am loved by the King,

CHORUS TAG:

    C   D   G
And it makes my heart want to sing.

VERSE 2:

    G   D/F♯
I will lift my eyes in the darkest night,

  Em⁷   C
For I know my Savior lives.

   D   G
And I will walk with You

         D/F♯
Knowing You see me through,

 Em⁷   D/F♯   G   Em⁷   C
And sing   the   songs You   give.

(REPEAT CHORUS & CHORUS TAG)

CONTINUED...

BRIDGE:

    Am⁷   G/B   C   D
I can sing in the troubled times, sing when I win.

    Am⁷   G/B
I can   sing when I lose my step

       C   D
and I   fall down a - gain.

    Am⁷   G/B
I can   sing 'cause You pick me up,

C   D
Sing 'cause You're there.

    Am⁷   G/B
I can   sing 'cause You hear me Lord,

       C   D
When I   call to You in pray - er.

    Am⁷   G/B
I can   sing with my last breath,

C   D   Am⁷   G/B
  Sing for I know that I'll   sing with the angels,

       C   D
And the saints around the throne.

(REPEAT CHORUS)

ENDING:

      C   D
And it makes my heart,

      C   G/B
I am loved by the King,

      C   D
And it makes my heart,

      C   G/B
I am loved by the King,

      C   D   G
And it makes my heart want to sing.

Yeah, I can sing.

Let God Arise

CHRIS TOMLIN, ED CASH and JESSE REEVES

KEY OF (A)

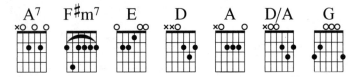

Capo 2 (A)

CONTINUED...

VERSE 1:

          A⁷
Hear the ho - ly roar of God resound,

Watch the waters part before us now.

          F#m⁷
Come and see   what He has done for us,

    E
Tell the world of His great love,

VERSE 2:

          A⁷
His en - emies will run for sure,

The church will stand, She will endure.

          F#m⁷
He holds   the keys of life, our Lord,

        E
Death has no sting, no final word,

PRE-CHORUS:

      D   F#m⁷   E
Our God is a God   who saves.

      D   F#m⁷   E
Our God is a God   who saves.

(REPEAT PRE-CHORUS)

(REPEAT CHORUS TWICE)

CHORUS:

        A   D/A
Let God arise, Let God arise.

        A⁷
Our God reigns now and forever,

     D/A
He reigns now and forever.

(G A⁷ D   G A⁷ D) *1st time only*

INSTRUMENTAL:

D F#m⁷ E   D F#m⁷ E

(REPEAT PRE-CHORUS TWICE)

(REPEAT CHORUS TWICE)

ENDING:

G A⁷   D   G A⁷   D

G A⁷   D   G A⁷   D

A

Let Your Mercy Rain

CHRIS TOMLIN, ED CASH and JESSE REEVES

KEY OF (C)

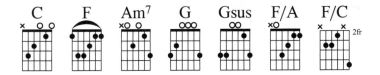

VERSE:

C   F   C
God, You have done great things,

     F   C
God, You give grace to the weak,

     F   Am⁷
And bless the brokenheart - ed,

        G
With a song   of praise to sing.

PRE-CHORUS:

        F   C
You reached down and lifted us up,

      F   C
You came running, looking for us.

        F
And now there's nothing,

   Am⁷   Gsus   G
And no   one beyond Your love.

CHORUS 1:

        C
You're the o - verflow,

      F   F/A
You're the foun - tain of my heart.

   G
So let Your mercy rain,

   F   C
Let Your mercy rain on us.

(REPEAT VERSE)

(REPEAT PRE-CHORUS)

(REPEAT CHORUS 1)

CONTINUED...

CHORUS 2:

C
You're the faithful one,

            F   F/A
When the world's falling apart.

        G
So let Your mercy rain,

      F   C   *(last time F/C)*
Let Your mercy rain on us.

BRIDGE:

       Am⁷   G/B   C
How deep,   how wide,   how long,

         F   C   F
How high is your love, is Your love?

       Am⁷   G/B   C
How deep,   how wide,   how long,

         F   C
How high is your love,

         F   C   F
is Your love,   Oh God?

(REPEAT CHORUS 1)

(REPEAT CHORUS 2 TWICE)

C   F/C   C

          F   C
Let it rain.

The Lion Became The Lamb

MATT MAHER and CHRIS TOMLIN

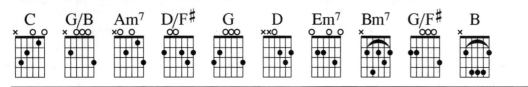

Capo 1 (C)

VERSE 1:

                C   G/B
It was in the dark   I heard You call - ing,

                Am⁷   D/F♯
A mighty voice   whisper my name.

    G/B C   G/B
A fire   in - side, a sweet sur - render,

   Am⁷   D/F♯
My eyes began to see the beauty of the Savior.

CHORUS:

   G
On altars of stone in the human heart,

      Am⁷
You laid   down Your life; You took our part.

    G/B   C
For the sin of the world, the ran - som of all,

CHORUS ENDING:

    D   Em⁷ Bm⁷
The Lion became the Lamb of God,

   C   D
The Lion became the Lamb of God.

(C Bm⁷ Am⁷   D/F♯) *1st time only*

VERSE 2:

             C   G/B
No greater love, no one but Je - sus,

              Am⁷   D/F♯
Could roll away,   roll away the night.

    G/B C   G/B
Emman - uel, the gift of heav - en,

    Am⁷
You've crushed the enemy.

      D/F♯
I'm alive   and I'm forgiven.

CONTINUED...

(REPEAT CHORUS & CHORUS ENDING)

BRIDGE:

G   Am⁷   D/F♯
  And the time had come, though the war was won,

               G   G/F♯
The bat - tle for my free - dom

          Em⁷
had just   begun

                    Am⁷
But You wouldn't aban - don me

B   C
  for the sake of Your sto - ry.

(REPEAT CHORUS)

CHORUS TAG:

    G/B   D
The Lion became the Lamb.

(REPEAT CHORUS)

ENDING:

      D
The Lion became the Lamb.

You are seated at the Father's right hand.

The Lion became the Lamb of God.

C Bm⁷ Am⁷   D   G

Made To Worship

CHRIS TOMLIN, STEPHAN SHARP and ED CASH

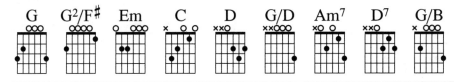

G   G2/F#   Em   C   D   G/D   Am7   D7   G/B

Capo 4 (G)

VERSE 1:

   G   G2/F#
Be - fore the day, be - fore the light,
   Em   C   D
Be - fore the world revolved around the sun.
G   G2/F#
God on high stepped down in   -   to time,
               Em
And wrote the sto - ry
                          C   D
of His love for everyone.

PRE-CHORUS:

C   D
  He has filled our hearts with wonder,
C   G/D   C
  so that we al - ways re - member:

CHORUS:

G
You and I were made to worship,
C
You and I are called to love,
Am7   D7
You and I are forgiven and free.
   G
When you and I embrace surrender,
   C
When you and I choose to believe,
   Am7   D7
Then you and I will see

(you and I will see) *3rd time only*

who we were meant to be.

VERSE 2:

G   G2/F#
  All we are and all we have,
   Em   C
Is all a gift from God that we receive.
G   G2/F#
Brought to life we open up   our eyes,
          Em   C   D
To see the maj - esty and glory of the King.

CONTINUED...

(REPEAT PRE-CHORUS)

(REPEAT CHORUS)

BRIDGE:

Am7
  Even the rocks cry out,
G/B
  even the heavens shout,
C   D7
  At the sound of His Holy name.
Am7
  So let every voice sing out,
G/B
  let every knee bow down,
C   D7
  He is worthy of all our praise.

(REPEAT CHORUS TWICE)

ENDING:

        C   Am7   D7
Yeah,   we were meant to be,   oo.
                    G   C   Am7   D7
You and I,   you and I,
                                  G
We were meant to be.

Over Me
CHRIS TOMLIN and SETH WALKER

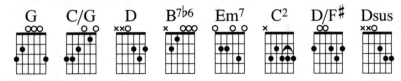

Capo 3 (G)

CONTINUED...

VERSE 1:

G   C/G   G
  Father hold me like a new born child,

D   G
  Father hold me like a new born child,

    B$^{7\flat6}$ Em^7 D   C^2
Father calm me when I   run   wild,

G   D   G
Father, watch over me.

VERSE 2:

G   C/G   G
  Father cool me when the fever's high,

D   G
  Father cool me when the fever's high,

    B$^{7\flat6}$ Em^7 D   C^2
Father show me through Je   -   sus' eyes,

     G   D   G
And Father, watch over me.

CHORUS:

    C^2 G
Over me, like the rain come down.

    D   G
Over me, how sweet the sound.

    C^2 G   D/F$^\sharp$ Em^7
Over me, angels gath - ered   round.

C^2 Dsus   G
Father, watch over me.

VERSE 3:

G   C/G   G
  Father call me to Your loving side,

D   G
  Father call me to Your loving side,

    B$^{7\flat6}$ Em^7 D   C^2
Father speak to me and I'll be   al - right,

     G   D   G
And Father, watch over me.

(REPEAT CHORUS)

GUITAR SOLO:

C^2 G   D   G   C^2

G   D/F$^\sharp$ Em^7 C^2 G

(REPEAT CHORUS)

ENDING:

C^2 Dsus   G   C/G   G
Father, watch over me.

Rejoice

CHRIS TOMLIN, ED CASH and JESSE REEVES

KEY OF (A)

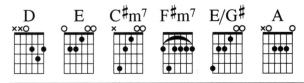

D   E   C#m⁷   F#m⁷   E/G#   A

CONTINUED...

VERSE 1:

    D
See the morning,

    E   C#m⁷   F#m⁷
See it rising over the mountains high.

    D
See the mercy

    E   F#m⁷   E/G#   A
in the mighty hand of God.

    D   E
Living water come and fill us,

  C#m⁷   F#m⁷
Only You can satis - fy.

      D   E   D   E
Turn our sorrow into singing the song of   Life.

CHORUS:

    A   E/G#   F#m⁷   D
Re - joice, re - joice, and sing with the angel voices.

    A   E/G#
Re - joice, re - joice,

  F#m⁷   D
all Heaven and earth re - joice.

(A   D   A   D) *1st time only*

VERSE 2:

            E
Lord Your strength is a tower,

  C#m⁷   F#m⁷
The righteous run in - to.

      D   E   F#m⁷ E/G# A
Lord Your love is a banner over us.

      D   E
And we hold on to the promise,

    C#m⁷   F#m⁷
That Your hold on us is true.

      D   E
There's no other like You Jesus,

    D   E
No one like   You.

(REPEAT CHORUS TWICE)

BRIDGE:

    E   C#m⁷
Al - ways, again I say re - joice.

     F#m⁷   D
Al - ways, again I say re - joice.

    E   C#m⁷
Al - ways, again I say re - joice.

  F#m⁷   D
Al - ways, al - ways.

(REPEAT CHORUS TWICE)

A D A D A D

Uncreated One

CHRIS TOMLIN and J.D. WALT

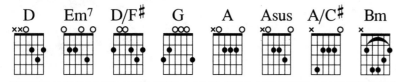

Capo 1 (D)

VERSE 1:

D Em⁷ D/F♯ G A D
Ho - ly   Uncre - at - ed One,

   G   D/F♯   Asus A
Your beauty fills   the skies.

       D A/C♯ Bm   Asus
But the glory of   Your majes - ty

     G   Asus A   D
Is the mercy in   Your eyes.

VERSE 2:

   D Em⁷ D/F♯ G A D
And wor - thy   Uncre - at - ed One,

   G   D/F♯   Asus A
From heaven to earth come down.

    D A/C♯ Bm   Asus
You laid a - side Your royal - ty

   G   Asus A   D
To wear the sin - ner's crown.

CHORUS 1:

    A   G D
And O Great God be glori - fied,

    A   G A   D
Our lives laid down, Your's magnified.

    A   G A Bm
And O Great God be lift - ed   high,

G   Asus A D
There is none   like You.

(D Bm Asus A   D   Bm Asus A)
(1st time only)

VERSE 3:

D Em⁷ D/F♯ G A   D
Je - sus, Savior, God's own son,

G   D/F♯   Asus A
Risen, reign - ing Lord.

     D A/C♯ Bm   Asus
Sus-tainer of the Universe

     G   Asus A   D
By the power of   Your word.

CONTINUED...

(REPEAT CHORUS 1)

CHANNEL:

D   Bm   Asus A   D   Bm

Asus   A   D   Bm
There is none like You,

Asus   A   D   Bm Asus A
There is none like You,

VERSE 4:

    D Em⁷ D/F♯ G   A   D
And when we   see Your match - less face,

   G   D/F♯   Asus   A
In speechless awe   we'll   stand.

    D   A/C♯ Bm   Asus
And there we'll bow with grateful   hearts,

     G   Asus A D
Un - to the Great   I Am.

CHORUS 2:

    A   G D
And O Great God be glori - fied,

    A   G A   D
Our lives laid down, Your's magnified.

    A   G A Bm
And O Great God be lift - ed   high,

G   Asus A Bm
There is none   like You.

G   Asus A D
There is none   like You.

ENDING:

Bm Asus A   D

Bm   Asus   A   D
        There is none like You,

Bm Asus A   D   Bm Asus A   D

Amazing Grace (My Chains Are Gone)

JOHN NEWTON, JOHN P. REES and EDWIN OTHELLO EXCELL
Arrangement and additional chorus CHRIS TOMLIN and LOUIE GIGLIO

Amazing Grace, how sweet the sound,
That saved a wretch like me.
I once was lost, but now I'm found,
Was blind but now I see.

'Twas Grace that taught my heart to fear,
And Grace my fears relieved.
How precious did that Grace appear,
The hour I first believed.

My chains are gone, I've been set free,
My God, my Savior has ransomed me.
And like a flood His mercy reigns,
Unending love, Amazing Grace.

The Lord has promised good to me,
His word my hope secures.
He will my shield and portion be,
As long as life endures.

The earth shall soon dissolve like snow,
The sun forbear to shine.
But God who called me here below,
Will be forever mine,
Will be forever mine,
You are forever mine.

Awesome Is The Lord Most High

CHRIS TOMLIN, JESSE REEVES, CARY PIERCE and JON ABEL

Great are You, Lord, mighty in strength.
You are faithful, and You will ever be.
We will praise You all of our days,
It's for Your glory, we offer everything.

Raise your hands all you nations,
Shout to God all creation,
How awesome is the Lord most high.

Where You send us, God we will go.
You're the answer, we want the world to know.
We will trust You when You call our name,
Where You lead us, we'll follow all the way.

We will praise You together,
For now and forever.
How awesome is the Lord most high.

Hallelujah, hallelujah,
How awesome is the Lord most high.

Enough
CHRIS TOMLIN and LOUIS GIGLIO

You are my supply, my breath of life,
And still more awesome than I know.
You are my reward worth living for,
And still more awesome than I know.

And all of You is more than enough for all of me,
For every thrist and every need.
You satisfy me with Your love,
And all I have in You is more than enough.

You're my sacrifice of greatest price,
And still more awesome than I know.
You're the coming King, You are everything,
And still more awesome than I know.

More than all I want, more than all I need,
You are more than enough for me.
More than all I know, more than all I can see,
You are more than enough.

Everlasting God

BRENTON BROWN and KEN RILEY

Strength will rise as we wait upon the Lord,
We will wait upon the Lord,
We will wait upon the Lord,

Our God, You reign forever,
Our hope, our Strong Deliverer.

You are the everlasting God,
The everlasting God,
You do not faint,
You won't grow weary.

You're the defender of the weak,
You comfort those in need,
You lift us up on wings like eagles.

Glorious
CHRIS TOMLIN and JESSE REEVES

We lift our hands in praise to You,
We lift our hearts in worship to You, Lord.
We lift our voice to You and sing,
Our greatest love will ever be You, Lord.

Glorious, over us,
You shall reign glorious.

There is a King that we adore,
With humble hearts we bow before You, Lord.
There is a place we long to be,
Face to face we long to see You, Lord.

Majesty and power,
Are Yours alone forever.

Glory In The Highest

CHRIS TOMLIN, ED CASH, MATT REDMAN, JESSE REEVES and DANIEL CARSON

You are the first, You go before,
You are the last, Lord You're the encore.
Your name's in lights for all to see,
The starry host declare Your glory.

Glory in the highest,
Glory in the highest,
Glory in the highest.

Apart from You there is no God,
Light of the world, the bright and morning star.
Your name will shine for all to see,
You are the one, You are my glory.

And no one else could ever compare to You, Lord.
All the earth together declare:
Glory in the highest, to You Lord.

All the earth will sing Your praise,
The moon and stars, the sun and rain.
Every nation will proclaim,
That You are God and You will ransom.

Glory, glory Hallelujah,
Glory, glory to You Lord.
Glory, glory Hallelujah, Hallelujah.

How Can I Keep From Singing

CHRIS TOMLIN, MATT REDMAN and ED CASH

There is an endless song, echoes in my soul,
I hear the music ring.
And though the storms may come, I am holding on,
To the rock I cling.

How can I keep from singing Your praise,
How can I ever say enough?
How amazing is Your love?
How can I keep from shouting Your name?
I know I am loved by the King,
And it makes my heart want to sing.

I will lift my eyes in the darkest night,
For I know my Savior lives.
And I will walk with You knowing You'll see me through,
And sing the songs You give.

I can sing in the troubled times, sing when I win.
I can sing when I lose my step, and fall down again.
I can sing 'cause You pick me up, sing 'cause You're there.
I can sing 'cause You hear me, Lord, when I call You in prayer.
I can sing with my last breath, sing for I know,
That I'll sing with the angels and the saints around the throne.

Let God Arise

CHRIS TOMLIN, ED CASH and JESSE REEVES

Hear the holy roar of God resound,
Watch the waters part before us now.
Come and see what He has done for us,
Tell the world of His great love,
Our God is a God who saves.
Our God is a God who saves.

Let God arise, Let God arise.
Our God reigns now and forever,
He reigns now and forever.

His enemies will run for sure,
The church will stand, She will endure.
He holds the keys of life, our Lord,
Death has no sting, no final word,
Our God is a God who saves,
Our God is a God who saves.

Let Your Mercy Rain

CHRIS TOMLIN, ED CASH and JESSE REEVES

God, You have done great things,
God, You give grace to the weak,
And bless the brokenhearted,
With a song of praise to sing.

You reached down and lifted us up,
You came running, looking for us.
And now there's nothing,
And no one beyond Your love.

You're the overflow,
You're the fountain of my heart.
So let Your mercy rain,
Let Your mercy rain on us.
You're the faithful one,
When the world's falling apart.
So let Your mercy rain,
Let Your mercy rain on us.

How deep, how wide, how long,
How high is Your love, is Your love?
How deep, how wide, how long,
How high is Your love, is Your love, Oh God?

The Lion Became The Lamb

MATT MAHER and CHRIS TOMLIN

It was in the dark I heard You calling,
A mighty voice whisper my name.
A fire inside, a sweet surrender,
My eyes began to see the beauty of the Savior.

On altars of stone in the human heart,
You laid down Your life; You took our part.
For the sin of the world, the ransom of all,
The Lion became the Lamb of God,
The Lion became the Lamb of God.

No greater love, no one but Jesus,
Could roll away, roll away the night.
Emmanuel, the gift of heaven,
You've crushed the enemy.
I'm alive and I'm forgiven.

And the time had come, though the war was won,
The battle for my freedom had just begun.
But You wouldn't abandon me for the sake of Your story.

Made To Worship

CHRIS TOMLIN, STEPHAN SHARP and ED CASH

Before the day, before the light,
Before the world revolved around the sun.
God on high stepped down into time,
And wrote the story of His love for everyone.

He has filled our hearts with wonder,
So that we always remember:

You and I were made to worship,
You and I are called to love,
You and I are forgiven and free.
When you and I embrace surrender,
When you and I choose to believe,
Then you and I will see who we were meant to be.

All we are and all we have,
Is all a gift from God that we receive.
Brought to life, we open up our eyes,
To see the majesty and glory of the King.

Even the rocks cry out, even the heavens shout,
At the sound of His holy name.
So let every voice sing out, let every knee bow down,
He is worthy of all our praise.

Over Me

CHRIS TOMLIN and SETH WALKER

Father hold me like a new born child,
Father hold me like a new born child,
Father calm me when I run wild,
Father, watch over me.

Father cool me when the fever's high,
Father cool me when the fever's high,
Father show me through Jesus' eyes,
And Father, watch over me.

Over me, like the rain come down.
Over me, how sweet the sound.
Over me, angels gathered round.
Father, watch over me.

Father call me to Your loving side,
Father call me to Your loving side,
Father speak to me and I'll be alright,
And Father, watch over me.

Rejoice

CHRIS TOMLIN, ED CASH and JESSE REEVES

See the morning,
See it rising over the mountains high.
See the mercy in the mighty hand of God.
Living water come and fill us,
Only You can satisfy.
Turn our sorrow into singing the song of Life.

Rejoice, rejoice, and sing with the angel voices.
Rejoice, rejoice, all Heaven and earth rejoice.

Lord Your strength is a tower,
The righteous run in to.
Lord Your love is a banner over us.
And we hold on to the promise,
That Your hold on us is true.
There's no other like You Jesus,
No one like You.

Always, again I say rejoice.

Uncreated One
CHRIS TOMLIN and J.D. WALT

Holy Uncreated One, your beauty fills the skies.
But the glory of Your majesty is the mercy in Your eyes.

And worthy Uncreated One, from heaven to earth come down.
You laid aside Your royalty to wear the sinner's crown.

And O Great God be glorified,
Our lives laid down, Your's magnified.
And O Great God be lifted high,
There is none like You.

Jesus, Savior, God's own son, Risen, reigning Lord.
Sustainer of the Universe by the power of Your word.

And when we see Your matchless face,
In speechless awe we'll stand.
And there we'll bow with grateful hearts,
Unto the Great I Am.

YOUR
SEARCH IS OVER . . .
WORSHIP TOGETHER.com®
NEW SONGS FAVORITE SONGS
ALL IN ONE PLACE
HERE I AM TO WORSHIP
BLESSED BE YOUR NAME
FOREVER
HOW GREAT IS OUR GOD
HOLY IS THE LORD
EVERLASTING GOD
IN CHRIST ALONE
THERE IS A REDEEMER
HOW MAJESTIC IS YOUR NAME
I COULD SING OF YOUR LOVE FOREVER
For all your music resources including transposable CHORD CHARTS, SHEET MUSIC, NEW SONG CAFÉ INSTRUCTIONAL VIDEOS and more, visit WORSHIP TOGETHER.com